SCALD

Date: 8/16/17

811.6 DUH
Duhamel, Denise,
Scald /

PITT POETRY
50 YEARS
SERIES

ED OCHESTER, EDITOR

SCALD

DENISE DUHAMEL

UNIVERSITY OF PITTSBURGH PRESS

Published by the University of Pittsburgh Press, Pittsburgh, Pa., 15260
Manufactured in the United States of America
Printed on acid-free paper
10 9 8 7 6 5 4 3 2 1

ISBN 13: 978-0-8229-6450-6
ISBN 10: 0-8229-6450-3

Cover art: Susan Osgood, *Hot Spot*, 1998. Oil on canvas, 73.5 × 57.7 in.
Cover design by Melissa Dias-Mandoly

For Kerri and Kate

CONTENTS

FOR SHULIE

How Deep It Goes   3
On the Occasion of Typing My First Email on a Brand-New Phone   12
Helen Hamilton Gardener's Brain   14
People-ing   18
Amazon   19
Darwinian Pantoum   23
Bikini Kill Villanelle   26
The Immortal Jellyfish   27
Conceptual Villanelle   29
Reproduction Pantoum   30

FOR ANDREA

Fornicating   37
Dogs   42
Sex Dream   43
Memoir   44
Reader/Writer   47
Rated R   48
Extreme Villanelle   54
Porn Poem (with Andrea Dworkin)   55
Canna   56
The Tenants of Feminism   59
Reading   60
Maybe Your East Village Was Better Than Mine: A Braided Poem   62

FOR WICKEDARY MARY

Safety Pantoum   71

Our Lady of the Milk   73

Distinguished   78

Snake Pantoum   79

Scalding Cauldron   81

The End Is Coming   83

Humanity 101   85

Castrati of the Eighteenth Century   87

What Child Is This?   88

Pilgrims   92

Americas   93

Filling Station, 2012   95

Recycling   97

The Things That Never Can Come Back   98

Acknowledgments   101

FOR SHULIE

SHULAMITH FIRESTONE

(JANUARY 7, 1945–AUGUST 28, 2012)

HOW DEEP IT GOES

I loved Shulie for writing
that giving birth
is like "shitting a pumpkin"

and that childhood
is a "supervised nightmare."
It was easy for me to decide

I didn't want kids. Reared
on Andrea Dworkin, it was also easy
to rule out intercourse:

can an occupied people—
physically occupied inside,
internally invaded—be free?

When Dworkin died in 2005,
an anchor on Fox made a crude joke
and Cathy Young called her *a 'sad ghost'*

that feminism needs to exorcise.
Some of us knew Dworkin
was onto something,

but Shulamith Firestone knew
we'd probably shut it down:
Feminists have to question

not just all of Western culture,
but the organization of culture itself,
and further, even the very organization

of nature. Many women give up in despair:
if that's how deep it goes
they don't want to know…

which leads me to women
who want children, which leads me
to women who get three months

parental leave and that's it.
I'm talking about the U.S. in 2015,
but what about China

where foot binding was legal until 1912,
which leads me to human history.
Plato wasn't down with women's rights

as *such a shift could alter the household*
and the state. And Aristotle
thought women's work had no value.

The Enlightenment was not so enlightened
when it came to women,
which leads me to searching for historical blips

of female equality—
Spartan women got some glory
if their sons were warriors.

Those moms could own land
and take care of estates.
In third century BCE, Stoics

believed that men and women
should wear the same clothing,
enter marriage, not as a biological

imperative, but as equals.
Stoics had a good eight-hundred-year run
until, deemed pagan by Christians,

all their schools were shut down.
Quakers believed women and men
were spiritually one and the same.

Margaret Fell, in 1668, wrote
"Women's Speaking Justified,"
arguing for a female ministry.

In 1782, before the word feminism
came into being, Mary Wollstonecraft
pled her case in *A Vindication*

of the Rights of Woman—
that marriage should be between
two partners, not a father-husband

and a vain child-wife who sacrifices her life
to "libertine notions of beauty."
Which leads me to New Zealand in 1893,

the first of many countries
to give women the right to vote.
The ERA put up a good, yet losing, fight.

Birth control, 1975 declared
International Women's Year—
which leads me to Rush's feminazi.

Phyllis Schlafly. The Moral Majority.
The post-feminist label.
Rape as genocide—

500,000 women, in 1994, in Rwanda.
Dworkin again: *can those without*
a biologically based physical integrity

have self-respect?
Which leads me to Rousseau
and his "natural law,"

that certain men (white)
are superior to women
and all people of other races

because men are "rational animals,"
which leads me to men
and their rational wars,

which leads me to the animal kingdom—
the lion that kills the cubs
of his predecessor,

the male seed beetle with his barbed penis,
gangs of bottled-nosed dolphins
kidnapping females—

which leads me back to Shulie's despair.
It's a good thing women are long-term thinkers,
because it's going to take a while

until feminism is no longer a theory, but a reality,
says reluctant feminist Nancy Hopkins
cancer researcher at MIT,

which leads me to plastic surgery
or *The Death of Feminism*
which leads me to Pink's "Stupid Girls"

which leads me to fashion
and Madonna and Naomi Wolf,
which leads me to heterosexist privilege

which leads me to *Queer Futurity*
and José Esteban Muñoz
who dismisses the fight for same-sex marriage—

who would want to be part
of such a corrupt system?—
which leads me to women

in combat—why would women
want to shoot anybody else,
as they are so often victims of violence

themselves?—which leads me
to something like Female Futurity.
Should women dismiss

the fight for political representation
since it's all a sham? Should
women stop paying their taxes?

Should they eschew money
entirely and trade in
their lipsticks

and bras, their heels,
their hair dye?
Which leads me to the phrase

"having it both ways,"
a phrase I hate
as men always have it both ways

all ways, actually, always, actually,
which leads me to the false binaries
of gender which one would think

make feminism obsolete.
Pop androgyny pretty much died
with Annie Lenox and Grace Jones.

I remember kids dressing up
as Boy George
for Halloween in 1983

which brings me back
to Shulie's pumpkins
and a time of the Culture Club's

beloved innocence.
("I prefer a nice cup of tea to sex,"
said The Boy.) My unproven theory—

mainstream androgyny died
with AIDS. Gender-bending
was OK until it was labeled gay,

until HIV, until toddlers
with drawn-on eyebrows
scared their parents,

which leads me to polysexuality,
the trans world, cissexual
assumption, and though not

mainstream, pansexuality,
which Shulie thought was coming
and may be coming still

which leads me back to homophobia,
xenophobia, anorexia, mania,
which leads me to schizophrenia

from which Shulie suffered,
which leads me to her delusion—
people hiding behind masks

made of their very own faces,
which sounds poetic and apt to me—
which leads me

to mascara which leads me
to Louis Sass's definition
of the schizophrenic

as one who is *acutely aware*
of the inauthenticities and compromises
of normal social existence—

which leads me to John Keats
and his "negative capability,"
which leads me to, of all people,

F. Scott Fitzgerald
who, rephrasing Keats, wrote
The test of a first-rate intelligence

is the ability to hold two opposing ideas
in mind at the same time
and still retain the ability to function

which leads me—
If that's how deep it goes
do you want to know?—to you.

ON THE OCCASION OF TYPING MY FIRST
EMAIL ON A BRAND-NEW PHONE

When I sign "Denise,"
autocorrect suggests Denise Richards
which makes my ex-husband Charlie Sheen,
which makes me a mother of three daughters,
and sometimes more, as I also volunteer
to take care of the twins
Charlie fathered with his third wife Brooke Mueller
while she's in rehab.
In my new identity, I'm ten years younger,
a lot skinnier, but I haven't read much.
In my new identity, I get breast implants
so I can be in *Wild Things*
for which I become pretty famous
because of a sex scene with Neve Campbell in a pool.
But after that, my acting goes nowhere
except for bit parts and my now-cancelled reality show
It's Complicated, which only runs for a year,
and for which Charlie calls me "greedy and vain."
Sure, I get to be in *The World is Not Enough*,
but *Entertainment Weekly* rates me
the worst Bond Girl of all time.
In my new identity, I still have a sister named Michelle.
I'm still French Canadian, raised Roman Catholic.
I still get to be a writer, but when I'm Denise Richards,
instead of poems, I publish a memoir
The Real Girl Next Door.
I'm a *New York Times* bestseller,
but deep down I know
it's not because I wield a great sentence.
In my new identity, instead of overeating,

I get more plastic surgery and pose for *Playboy*
when my marriage heads south
and I no longer "feel sexy"
and just want to "prove something."
In my new identity, my mother has passed,
but my father is still alive
going to *The Millionaire Matchmaker*
to look for new love. Though I'm no
genius, I'm generally respected
because I don't badmouth anyone,
even when I'm on Howard Stern.
I repeatedly decline to talk
about the restraining order
or any of Sheen's public subsequent meltdowns.
What's the point? Besides, I need to protect my kids.
There aren't many famous Denise's,
and I wonder why my phone, if it's that "smart,"
doesn't suggest Levertov. When I erase Richards,
autocorrect still doesn't recognize who I am.
As I try to re-sign, Samsung asks
if I'm sure I'm just a plain old Denise.
Might I really mean "Denies"
or maybe "Demise?"

HELEN HAMILTON GARDENER'S BRAIN

She donated her brain
to Cornell to prove once and for all
there was no difference between the sexes
and their neurological functions.

Indeed, Cornell proved once and for all
how smart Gardener was, but attributed
her superior neurological functions
to her race, class, and education.

How smart she was! *The New York Times*
ran "The Human Brain Still Puzzles Scientists,"
detailing Gardener's race, class, and education.
Gardener had turned to science

even though she knew scientists were only human—
thus her debate with the surgeon general.
Women had turned to science
after, she wrote, *hell went out of fashion.*

In 1888, she debated with the surgeon general
whose findings were full of prejudice and sexism.
She wrote, *After hell went out of fashion....*
It was no longer her soul, but her body

that would be met with prejudice and sexism.
After Darwinism, scientists were the new priests—
It was no longer her soul, but her body,
that needed saving from herself.

After Darwinism, scientists were the new priests,
noting sex-based differences in the brain.
Apparently, a women needed saving from
her pea brain that weighed less than a man's.

Noting sex-based differences in the brain,
the surgeon general was against higher education
for women with their pea brains,
who were surely incapable of sustained abstract thought.

Scientists were also against higher education
for the poor and blacks. But it was scientists
who were incapable of broad-minded thought—
they said girls' nervous systems would be ruined by math.

When it came to poor blacks, scientists
argued those populations, too, had smaller brains—boys' and
girls' nervous systems could be ruined by math.
Even Gardener herself fell into the trap,

arguing with data that proved women had smaller brains
by pointing out scientists had only studied female "tramps."
Even Gardener fell into the trap—
of course, Byron's brain outweighed a woman's

if scientists only studied female "tramps."
Gardener became obsessed—
of course, Byron's brain outweighed a woman's
if that woman wasn't Elizabeth Cady Stanton.

Gardener became obsessed—
rallying smart women to donate their brains.
It wasn't that Elizabeth Cady Stanton
refused, but her heirs did and buried her,

brain and all, unwilling to donate their smart mother.
Helen Hamilton Gardener had no children
to refuse, no immediate heirs to stop her wishes
so her own postmortem brain could testify on her behalf.

Helen Hamilton Gardener had no children
to usher in the flapper generation,
so her own postmortem brain could testify on her behalf
in October 1927, two years before the Great Depression.

Did the flapper generation even notice—
those bobbed women and dandy men?
In October 1927, two years before the Great Depression,
the brain debate was put to rest.

Many bobbed women and dandy men
were having too much fun to be interested in biology,
the brain debate put to rest.
Stanton wrote, *If there was no Fall,*

women might have been less interested in biology.
Gardener looked to science for truth.
Stanton wrote, *If there was no Fall,*
there was no need of a Savior.

Gardener looked to science for truth—
proof there was no difference between the sexes.
Perhaps there was no need for her to play Savior.
Still, she donated her brain.

PEOPLE-ING

A small group of birds are fascinated with us—
our vocal humming and mechanical honks, our echolalia
and rages, our pop tunes and symphonies.
These birds watch us in our natural environments,
the common cluster of the tops of our heads, hoping
to see a truly remarkable and rare human,
someone performing telekinesis or being struck by lightning
and then surviving. When they migrate, birds
differentiate the languages of the human species
in Florida and Cuba, then Jamaica. These birds wonder
if we can understand each other. If we understand
our dogs, and if our dogs understand the squirrels.
People-ers keep detailed lists, dated with the times
their humans were spotted. Most birds come to the birdfeeder
simply to peer into our windows.
They flutter near delivery rooms, hoping to show
their chicks a human birth
as a way to ease them into a discussion of sex.
If a bird dreams its feet are heavy, rooting it to the ground,
such a dream indicates creativity.
Some birds are working on a plan to lure one of us
into a giant cage with just a bed and a mirror
into which the captured human can preen.
Are birds freaked out when they see one of us
eat one of them? Is that why they fly so low at picnics?
Is that why they shit on our cars?

AMAZON

Whenever someone mentioned the word,
I first thought of amazon.com

even though I was in the real Amazon
canoeing in a lagoon under a glimpse of moon.

I held the tiny flashlight I'd bought online
though in truth the guides did all the hard work

paddling and winking their own lights twice
whenever they sensed something—bats, prehistoric

wild turkeys, Potoos who lay their eggs
in tree crooks. Each startling wing-whoosh.

The melon-sized bullfrog looked red in the dark.
We were there to see the glowworm's larvae

dazzle the night like strands of twinkle lights
festooned in their own geometry. Before I left home

I'd read an essay by Arielle Greenberg—*the ethical
travel poem is perhaps the most difficult to write.*

I'd read about Chevron's "Rainforest
Chernobyl," dumping toxins into rivers

people use for bathing. I spritzed myself
with DEET which couldn't have been good

for the ecosystem. I wondered about
the folly of the first European settlers

in this land of leeches and mosquitoes,
overgrown boughs dipping into tributaries,

monkeys leaping above, branch to branch—
on land, nests of flesh-eating ants.

I wondered about my own folly, my surprise
at nocturnal jungle sounds, nothing like white noise

machine settings. I jumped at each screech,
hiss, squawk, and chirp amplified in my cabin.

I had a net under which I could sleep and rubber
boots to protect me from snake bites,

but if you can believe Francisco de Orellana,
Amazon women warriors controlled the place

in 1541. He was looking for gold, and the warriors
let him pass, knowing he would find only rain

and disease. Now if you search Amazon
your first Google pages will list the store,

which makes a goldmine, appropriating
the name of Greek women warriors,

who are said to have cauterized their right breasts
to mesh with their bows, to better aim

their arrows. Francisco de Orellana also appropriated
their name in South America. Some say

these Amazons were "Virgins of the Sun," Incas
fleeing the rape of other Spanish conquerors

to the north. I was fleeing nothing, only fulfilling
a childhood Tarzan and Jane dream. Wanting

an experience, the ultimate cliché. Wanting
to write what I saw and wanting you to read,

even while acknowledging words are slippery
as mud covering the primary forest

where we'd hiked earlier in the day,
where we were too unsteady to even dare

take out our cameras. Where the earth
was taunting us, *Co-opt this*. Not one tourist

was able to capture the glowworms either,
the awe and ecstasy we felt flickering in nature

or, rather, our nature flickering in us. We tried
using our *oohs* and similes, the larvae radiant

as the vending machine of Coke glowing
back at the lodge. The larvae radiant

as an Amazonian marquee. Drunk on beauty,
someone said the larvae sparkled like Chablis.

The guide who spoke the most English said *yes,*
but the Amazon is not what it used to be.

DARWINIAN PANTOUM

Constant change, unlimited variation—
Adam and Eve kicked to the curb—
our real ancestors, not divine but animal.
In fact, we humans *are* animal.

Adam and Eve kicked to the curb,
the male's *power to charm*
(in fact, humans *are* animal)
more important than to conquer in battle.

In order to charm the females,
male animals strutted, sang, and puffed up
even more than in battle.
"Female choice" made women curious.

If males strutted, sang, and puffed up,
it was not in any world Victorians knew.
"Female choice" made women frown,
corsets jabbing into their ribs.

Victorian women knew they had to paint
their faces with white wax and spermaceti,
corsets jabbing into their ribs.
They swabbed their lips with dyed beeswax.

Faces painted with white wax and spermaceti,
Victorian women wooed the men.
Swabbing their lips with dyed beeswax,
women sought husbands only to find

Victorian men owned their wives' wombs.
Married women had no legal recourse.
They'd sought husbands only to find
a honeymoon of brutal assault.

A married woman had no legal recourse,
no right to her body, labeled "asexual."
After a honeymoon of brutal assault,
she might be labeled frigid or worse.

No right to her body, labeled "asexual,"
she might have read Darwin's *endless forms*.
Though labeled frigid or worse, she knew
animals *are being evolved*.

When she read of Darwin's *endless forms*
did she think of her daughters—
animals *being evolved?*
Did she think of future granddaughters?

Maybe she thought of her grandson
applying lampblack to lengthen his lashes.
Though stuck, she had hope for her granddaughters—
that they'd be better able to select their mates.

Applying lampblack to lengthen lashes
was messy and took a long time,
but women thought it necessary to secure mates.
Maybe someday marriage would look different.

Evolution was messy and took a long time.
A woman's real ancestors, not divine but animal.
Maybe someday marriage would look different—
constant change, unlimited variation.

BIKINI KILL VILLANELLE

Whatever happened to those Riot Grrrl
fanzines? Extra *r*'s slashed to "girl power,"
the growl softened by the mainstream Spice Girls

who, in black Wonderbras, spout faux pearls
of wisdom and flirt with Matt Lauer.
Whatever happened to those Riot Grrrls—

Tobi Vail's drums, Kathleen Hanna's snarls?
I put batteries in dancing flowers
that boogied down with the mainstream Spice Girls.

Kurt Cobain knew music's future was girls,
their pink/punk scalding fury and glower.
Whatever happened to those Riot Grrrls

happened to us, too. Revolution swirled
with sugar in blenders. We devoured
the stuff, sweetened by the mainstream Spice Girls.

Women do crunches, pushups and leg curls
so they'll look good at cocktail hour.
Whatever happened to those Riot Grrrls
who kicked open that door for the Spice Girls?

THE IMMORTAL JELLYFISH

for Nadra

A young poet tells me about a certain jellyfish that can go back to childhood, after it has already given birth—from parent to infant and then back again, its ninety stinging tentacles reverting to eight. Prey comes around—and suddenly the adult is a toddler, able to hide. Prey comes around—and suddenly the toddler is an adult, able to stand up for itself. When the jellyfish lifts its umbrella-body inside out, the past is the future, the future the past. The pulsating bell, a puff of red stomach marked with a cross. How can I not see a pregnant belly and the crucifix?

"I don't think I can handle it," the young poet says, about the metaphorical implications of *T. dohrnii,* so the jellyfish in her poem remain of the mortal variety. I wonder about arrested development, plastic surgery, Ponce de León. I wonder about adult pacifiers, teen moms, toddlers orphaned by war. Christ may have died for our sins, but what about the secular jellyfish, sinless in its shape-shifting, literally all instinct and nerve? And, given the chance, would we humans do what this jellyfish can? Go back and forth to play hide and seek or pay the mortgage? To remember, to forget, to remember again?

The answer is yes. We turn ourselves inside out and switch places—my student is a fifty-one-year old poet, and I, her undergraduate. Perhaps I have found a way at last to write about the immortal jellyfish. My student/now professor is humming, marking up my poem. I sit on the other side of her desk, anxious for approval, highlighting Wordsworth's ode to stay busy. The date pages of her calendar flutter, smudged, below a picture of the Virgin Mary of Guadalupe. My student/now professor says, "The real question you need to ask, traveling forever back and forth or not, is this…Will the earth always be here to accept us?"

Even the immortal jellyfish can succumb to disease, the pollution of the sea. Glory to the jellyfish for as long as it lasts, glory to our burdened planet and its famous umbrellas—Gene Kelly's, Mary Poppins', Rihanna's. Glory to the clear umbrella the young poet used in first grade, the ribs of which poked through the plastic dome. She tried to fight against the rain gusts and wind, but the handle tore from her grasp and the inverted umbrella tumbled like a bony ghost down the street. She is about to catch pneumonia that almost does her in. Glory to resurrection. I am six, and fifty-one, and also nineteen. In my lap, a bright yellow mark—*And the babe leaps up on his mother's arm.*

CONCEPTUAL VILLANELLE

You were never born, never conceived
but for my tame imagination—
my worst traits coupled with a lover's genes,

his ugly temper, my food allergies.
No chance to rebel, prodigal son,
since you were never born, never conceived.

No daughter to replicate my pet peeves,
no Snow White to hate me in the long run.
I never coupled with another's genes—

my vanity and insecurity,
his bravado and love of tommy guns—
you were never born, never conceived.

No cravings, no maternity leave.
My oven never concocted a bun
made of my worst traits and a lover's genes.

You'll never be told, *Grow up, you're naive.*
You'll never be taunted, never be shunned.
You were never born, never conceived.
I cursed all my dates. I buttoned my jeans.

REPRODUCTION PANTOUM

In the beginning was the sea,
all life-forms growing in the ocean.
In the beginning was the moon,
no gestation, no sperm, just tides—

all life-forms growing in the ocean,
a womb itself, primordial and marine.
No gestation, no sperm, just tides
of creatures born from embryos

in a sea's womb, primordial and marine.
In the beginning, before the beginning
of creatures born from embryos,
was a meteor, the moon already there

in the beginning. Before the beginning
of the solar system was the Milky Way,
which Aristotle praised in *Meteorologica*.
Before the universe itself—what?

Before the solar system was the Milky Way,
before that the Big Bang.
But before the universe itself—what?
A zero? A time before time even existed?

Before that Big Bang,
was there an infinity we just can't grasp?
Or a zero? A time before time even existed?
Is it presumptuous to think there's an answer?

Is there an infinity we just can't grasp?
Enough with the chicken and the egg.
Though presumptuous to think there's an answer,
modern science argues a non-chicken ancestor—

enough like a chicken to produce an egg—
see Stephen Hawking and Charles Darwin.
Modern science argues a non-human ancestor
for us, a generalized salty female existence—

see Stephen Hawking. Charles Darwin
connected the moon with menstruation,
a generalized salty female existence.
Both human and chick embryos have gills,

connecting the sea and moon. Menstrual
cycles developed from estrous ones.
Though human and chick embryos have gills,
neither humans nor chickens experience estrus.

Freed from their ancestors' estrous cycles,
women can have sex any time.
Neither humans nor chickens go into heat
though most ovulate regularly.

Women can have sex any time,
each with a clitoris designed for pleasure.
Though most ovulate regularly,
herbs and science help women to control pregnancies.

Each with a clitoris designed for pleasure
women can often be demonized, though
herbs and science allow them to control pregnancies.
This orgasmic potential for women

can often be demonized, though,
if we take the long view, it may not always be so.
The orgasmic potential for women
resides in the clitoris, no reproductive function.

If we take the long view, it may not always be so
crazy to consider evolving pleasure. Colobus monkeys
delight in the clitoris, no reproductive function,
just eight thousand nerve endings.

Consider the evolving pleasure of porcupines
rubbing against rocks and sticks to awake
those eight thousand nerve endings.
Not everything is about reproduction.

Rubbing against cocks or hands can awake
desire, a human's stellar explosion.
Not everything is about reproduction.
What about the survival of glee?

Desire—a stellar explosion
of stem cells, clones, frozen embryos.
What about the survival of glee?
True, the end may be coming soon—

stem cells, clones, frozen embryos,
all sly ways to trick our fate.
True, the end may be coming soon
for us, but what about the lunar currents,

the sly ways they trick our fate?
In the beginning was the moon,
and, for us, the lunar currents.
In the beginning was the sea.

FOR ANDREA

ANDREA DWORKIN

(SEPTEMBER 26, 1946–APRIL 9, 2005)

FORNICATING

such a beautiful
day
and I'm not
fornicating

—Adília Lopes

I have goose bumps
from the breeze
coming into the window
which is a kind of fornication
but who am I kidding
a breeze is not even a kiss
especially a breeze
strained through a screen

I would have a better chance
out on the street
where I could perhaps meet
someone who wanted
to fornicate
with me or someone like me
and I could pretend
I suppose
even to be someone else
give a fake name
so the man would never
find me again

it is a little scary to say
to a stranger, *Hey, do you
want to fornicate?*
especially if you are a woman
and you want to fornicate
with a man

what kind of a man
would say yes to such a request

maybe a violent one
maybe no decent man at all
since the request is pretty bold
and I suppose I would
look crazy

men are leery of crazy women
and I can't blame them

I could promise a man
that I wouldn't
stalk him or call him ever
that I am just in it
for the fornication
but would he believe me

even I don't really believe me

because what if the fornication
were a success and I woke up
the next morning
another beautiful day
and I wasn't satisfied
with just the memory
of fornication
and wanted another round

or what if it was lousy
outside
and since I'd given a fake name
insisting I didn't want to know his
I had to look for a new fornicator
this time while lugging an umbrella

this time I could look for a woman
with the same sad look I have
when I want to fornicate
and if she agreed
we could step out of the rain
into her apartment
it might not be as scary
as approaching another man
or as big a leap over a puddle

Anne Sexton wrote
Once I was beautiful. Now I am myself...
then Adília Lopes wrote
once I was beautiful now I'm myself
then I wrote
fornication is for all the beautiful
and unbeautiful selves
on both beautiful
and unbeautiful days

not that I knew what I meant
it's just that sometimes
it's easy to feel unbeautiful
when you have unmet desires
or embarrassed that you have
such desires at all

I once wrote about a lover
who would pet his cat
instead of me
and my friend said
this poem is too vulnerable
I feel as though I should throw a coat
over this poem

she was right of course
and I tore it up
I only remember it today
because in her author photo
Adília Lopes holds a cat

I am allergic to cats
the lover had to wash his hands
those many years ago
before he could touch me

Kurt Vonnegut wrote
that every character needs
to want something
even if that something
is only a glass of water

I want to fornicate

I get up from my chair
and press my face against
the cool screen
until there is a dirty grid on my cheek
as though I've slept
in fifty tiny beds

DOGS

Everyone who leaves me immediately gets a dog.
Everyone I've ever left does the same.
I'm not just talking boyfriends and husbands,
but also platonic roommates. Before I'm abandoned,
everyone says a version of *No biggie. Dogs*
are only trouble anyway. And, besides, who's
going to feed them when I'm traveling?
New friends, not yet tired of me,
walk by the pound, so many pink noses
at the glass, and say something like, *They're cute,*
but I'd rather have you! Even my younger sister
got a mutt the day after I moved to college, as though
she and my parents had been plotting all along.
Maybe, because of my allergies, I've been
compensating all these years—fetching bones
and slobbering and panting, waiting for a pat on the head.
Maybe I've been too loyal, too simple in my affection.
Maybe I've rolled over too many times, waiting
for a big hand to scratch my belly. I used to think
everyone was downplaying their adoration
of dogs to make me feel better.
Now I realize I was the dog.

SEX DREAM

As the snakes crawl up through the floorboard cracks
(the cracks between my subconscious and conscious mind?)
I poke them with a spoon, try to push them
back down under the house
where, through an opening in the wood,
I see a bowl of rotting fruit below
and one snake, then two,
then a bundle squirming. *Who would build a floor*
atop another floor and leave behind a bowl of fruit? I ask.
You did, the contractor says as I stare at the grains
swirling in the wood (the vulva?) and the dark
revelatory holes. Apparently
I'd wanted to live above it all.

MEMOIR

If only I'd been a call girl
or dominatrix in college,
I'd have a memoir by now.
I missed the open
audition casting extras
in Etta James's music video
"Avenue D" because I was afraid
to call in sick to my real job.
I left the loft on Houston
before the orgy began,
my false eyelashes lost
to the clutter of a medicine cabinet.
The apartments I never bought
and flipped mock me.
Each poem I compose that is not
a Top 40 hit, each poem
that is not a screenplay,
assures my obscurity.
I'd hoped to bring Del's Lemonade
to the Miami masses
via kiosk or truck. I sent away
for the franchise information
to sell the frozen treat.
First made with snow
in the caves of Italy, Del's
was a staple of my Rhode Island
childhood. When shove came
to pushcart, I didn't do it,
skittish about business loans.

I'd have a memoir by now,
but there's so much suspicion
surrounding a woman's truth.
To paraphrase Kathleen Hanna,
I'm going to step up to the plate
then someone else is going to say,
"Really? You did what?
I don't think so." I didn't start
a band like Bikini Kill. I sat
in the boat while everyone else
snorkeled. I resisted so many
things on principle.
So many times I wanted
to be outrageously political
but then lost my nerve.
I've lived a double life,
then a triple life. For a time
I was even a wife
which felt a bit like decades
at a costume party.
The sex worker
was once my friend.
She hated rich men in a way
I understood. She benefited
from the meanest
and loneliest of humankind.
Each of us would have a memoir by now
though we'd rather not say
what really happened

those nights when we thought
we were all alone, no one else
with a life
as splintered and cracked
as our own.

READER/WRITER

Lady Gaga says she truly cares about all her Little Monsters.
They send her fan videos, tell her about the bullying and the beatings
which makes me remember the woman who approached me
at KGB Bar. Her eyes wet, she said, *Your work has meant so much to me.*
As she told me she was bulimic, just released from the hospital,
I felt so far away, as though I should have started to cry too,
and I did cry, kind of, but it was a fake nervous cry because I was "on,"
performing a persona, I suppose. I was aware of the line
of people behind her, people waiting to have books signed—
that was so new to me, so weird itself. I said, *Thank you
for telling me,* which I knew was completely inadequate.
She was that someone I had hoped for since I started to write,
that someone my poetry had actually helped, yet in that moment
I flubbed it. If she had written to me, I could have written
back something heartfelt, grateful that a poem of mine
actually reached a person who needed it, a poem like a FedEx box.
The woman was disappointed, I could tell, as she slunk away.
I signed books and chitchatted with people who had clear boundaries—
how perhaps I knew so-and-so, or how I should really try
the soba noodles at Dojo's. The woman stood near a stool
with her arms crossed. I thought I could feel her stare,
but every time I looked her way, she was looking at the floor.
When I finished signing, I walked towards her to talk—
she looked at me, shook her head *no,* then fled down the stairs.
This was years before Lady Gaga, but I felt like a Mother Monster.

RATED R

RESTRICTED FOR LANGUAGE

Of course, I can never say what I really want to say because language itself is a straitjacket. Between love and desire are six hundred non-words that can only be grunted or painted or danced. This is not to imply that I have given up on trying to free myself and stretch. Nineteenth-century doctors thought reading novels—even non-scandalous ones—induced mental illness. Houdini claimed he dislocated his shoulder in order to escape his straitjacket, but that has since been proven false. I have often found that by employing wiggles, patience, and silence, a close-enough word will come along.

RESTRICTED FOR VIOLENCE

On September 11, 2001, Sandra Bradshaw called home to say that she and another flight attendant were boiling pots of water to throw at the terrorists. In the film *United 93*, male passengers storm the cockpit, but it is quite possible that Bradshaw and her friend were the ones responsible for crashing the plane into a reclaimed strip mine in Pennsylvania. CNN is full of stories of male heroism, but according to Susan Faludi's *Terror Dream*, scalding water is what very well might have saved the White House.

RESTRICTED FOR ACTION AND PERIL

The enforcers of the Hays code insisted that the animators of Disney's *Fantasia* cover the female centaurs in flowered bras.

RESTRICTED FOR ADULT ACTIVITY

Mortgage payments. Voting. Car insurance. Taking that car to the mechanic. Networking. Time in suburbia. Child-rearing. Matching dishes and place settings. Retirement accounts. Scrapbooks. Arguing about politics. Vacuum cleaners, lawn mowers. Wills, living wills. Dinner parties, flirtations. Loan modification. Mid-life meltdowns. Taxes. Marriage. Adultery. Shame. Cholesterol. Fiber. Sympathy cards. Renewing a driver's license. Squinting at small print.

RESTRICTED FOR CRUDE SEXUAL CONTENT

The Carnal Knowledge Quartet puts on a good show. The Masturbation Nation Celebration always receives a standing ovation. You can't go wrong with the Sixty Nine Chorus Line or the Coitus Ventriloquist. The Cunnilingus Olympics leaves everyone breathless. And you haven't really lived until you've seen Anal Sex Acrobats fly above Fellatio Bongos. What about the Seduction Jugglers? Or the Hickey Hypnotist? You just missed The Phone Sex Circus—and the Gangbang Parade. You'll enjoy the one-act play about foreplay, the Fisting Magician, and the Dirty Talk Impersonators. But we also understand some of our viewers are quite refined.

RESTRICTED FOR CRUDE SITUATIONS

Medical damage resulting from the BP oil spill of 2010 is capped as follows—cleanup workers, $60,000; residents living within one-half mile of the water, $900 to $36,000.

RESTRICTED FOR SUGGESTIVE MATERIAL

That lone purple flip-flop I tripped on in the park. Or the bankrupt Trump Tower in Hollywood, FL—200 units but only the same three windows lit each night.

RESTRICTED FOR HARD LANGUAGE

The Waste Land. The Wastebasket Land. The Waistband Land. The Pantywaist Land. The Waistcoat Land. The Waste Water Treatment Land. The Waist-Deep-In-It Land. The Haste-Makes-Waste Land. The Waste-Not-Want-Not Land. The Waste-No-Time Land. The Waste-Your-Breath Land.

RESTRICTED FOR ALCOHOL

Everyone agreed I looked the oldest, so my friends pushed me into the liquor store to buy Peppermint Schnapps, the drink we thought came with its own breath mint, so our parents couldn't possibly know what we'd done. The man behind the counter didn't ask for ID. *Have fun,* he winked, returning to his girly magazine. On the way out, I pocketed a pack of Slim Jims.

RESTRICTED FOR DISTURBING/STARTLING IMAGES

The ban (1991-2009) on photographing the coffins of American soldiers coming back from Afghanistan and Iraq. Blackhawk helicopters. Chinook helicopters. A dead child carried over a parent's shoulder. The astonishing beauty of certain eyes. The empty sockets where eyes have been blown out by a dirty bomb. Drones. IEDs. Halliburton's 39.5 billion dollars worth of contracts.

RESTRICTED FOR THEMATIC ELEMENTS

You are bending into the washing machine, trying to come clean about the past, a volcano of bubbles up to your ankles. In the dream your sudsy toes are enormous which means you want to move forward with your life.

RESTRICTED FOR HORROR

I dressed as Carrie one Halloween and made the pig's blood from red dye and Karo syrup that stained my skin for a week, that gave me a temporary strawberry patch on my neck. Two pink footprints on my woolly bathmat.

RESTRICTED FOR BLOODY HORROR

O, precious blood, the blood of Christ and every soldier who is torn open, spilling human blood. O holy wars and domestic abuse. *I'm doing this for you,* says Jesus, says the president who sends the soldier. Paternal blood, fathers and sons. Maternal blood and menstruation, childbirth and its gore.

RESTRICTED FOR STRONG HORROR

Shrimp born without eyes. Fish of all kinds with large pink masses hanging over their gills. Crabs with holes in their misshapen shells, crabs dying inside.

Blue crabs without claws. Fish covered in lesions. Mutagenic dispersants entering the genome. The official word from BP: "Seafood from the Gulf is among the most tested in the world, and, according to the FDA and NOAA, it is as safe now as it was before the accident."

RESTRICTED FOR SEXUALLY ORIENTED NUDITY

As H. G. Wells wrote, "Moral indignation is jealousy with a halo . . ."

RESTRICTED FOR EMOTIONAL INTENSITY

The Skinner Box rewards the animal inside for certain behaviors, punishing it for others. Its inventor B.F. Skinner predicted in 1962, "In the not-too-distant future, the motivational and emotional conditions of normal life will probably be maintained in any desired state through the use of drugs." His utopian novel, *Walden Two*, describes an almost conflict-free existence. Even though he was encouraged by Robert Frost, Skinner knew he'd never write the great American novel. He just hadn't experienced enough.

RESTRICTED FOR DRUG USE

high cholesterol / high glucose / glucose meter / glucose intolerance / intolerance to dairy / intolerance to wheat / dairy elimination diet / dairy free recipes / diet pills / diet blogs / pill cutters / pills under the tongue / cutters and bulimics / cutters and misfits / bulimics and addicts / bulimics and kleptomaniacs / addicted to violence / addicted to porn / violence against women / violent video games / women and guns / women and HIV / guns and hunting / guns and hormones / hunting for results / hunting for the highest high

RESTRICTED FOR TOBACCO USE

After research showed that American six-year-olds were as familiar with "Joe Camel" as they were with Mickey Mouse, the cigarette companies went elsewhere. In Albania, Marlboro Girls roam the streets, giving out free cigarettes to kids. British American Tobacco's "Project Z" sells single cigarettes to those in Central America who otherwise couldn't afford a whole pack. YouTube's star, Aldi, the Indonesian toddler who smoked and twirled his cigarette with aplomb, went to rehab before he was four. He threatens to start smoking again when his mother refuses to buy him certain toys.

RESTRICTED FOR DISCRIMINATION/BULLYING

Tub of lard. Four Eyes. Freak.
Drink bleach, you geek.
Loser. Slut. Pussy. Wimp.
I'm a pacifist. I'm going to pass my fist through your teeth.

RESTRICTED FOR ROUGH AND/OR PERSISTENT VIOLENCE

Ziad Jarrah, the suspected hijacker of United 93, lived on Harding Street in Hollywood, FL just a few miles from me. The mail carrier said he'd delivered lots of packages and books to Jarrah, assuming he was a student. On September 7, 2001, Mohamed Atta drank five Stolichnayas with orange juice at Shuckum's on Young Circle, a place where I'd been with friends. Atta boasted he was a pilot, then left a crappy tip, $3 on a $45 bill. For the rest of 2001, when I drove home from teaching, I avoided U.S. 1 Fitness, where the terrorists took martial arts training. Its sign boasted a red boxing glove. I was glad when it went out of business and became Cross Fit ATP where the clients jump rope and dead lift. One of the trainers wears a grey Infidel tee shirt.

RESTRICTED FOR FRIGHTENING SCENES

Sometimes I fear I am the literary equivalent of horror vacui, filling up pages with details, leery of white space. Sometimes when I talk I forget to pause, assaulting my friends like a sonic Book of Kells or Crumb cartoon. Horror vacui is often seen in the obsessive line drawings of psychiatric patients. I know what it's like to circle around, follow a line, loop and dive to find the right word. I could say more, but I voluntarily fold my arms across my chest and request you tie the straitjacket's sleeves behind my back.

EXTREME VILLANELLE

"Violence is born of the desire to escape oneself."

—Iris Murdoch

Our drones, called Predator and Reaper,
have killed at least four hundred civilians
as they wiped out "extremists," life cheaper

in the Middle East. In D.C., sleeper
cells sleep. It costs up to fourteen million
to make one drone, Predator or Reaper.

Our strikes kill mothers, their kids, street sweepers,
and hurried shoppers at spice pavilions.
Are *we* the "extremists"? Are drones cheaper

than putting "boots on the ground"? Beleaguered
soldiers tire like small town vaudevillians
while our drones, Predator and Reaper,

are jazzed golems. Like a beekeeper,
a grounded pilot sends drones on a mission
to gather "extremists." Corn syrup's cheaper

than honey, so each morning a woman steeps her
tea then adds "honey," a sweet shenanigan
mocking bees. We play the part of Grim Reaper,
extreme sport extremist, as she does taiji.

PORN POEM (WITH ANDREA DWORKIN)

goldfish porn/applesauce porn/graphic pornographic traffic/
Bono porn/popcorn porn/forlorn porn/aurora borealis porn/
orchid porn/grilled Portobello porn…*pornography as social control,*
a way of saying publicly to every woman who walks down the street:
avert your eyes…adorable bauble porn/discreet stinky feet porn/
spirit visitation porn…*look down, bitch, because when you look up*
you're going to see a picture of yourself being hung,
you're going to see your legs spread open…plastic water pistol porn/
porn extra dry with three olives/feather weight porn/
heating pad porn/blinking pink neon kink/
pigtail porn/horn of plenty porn/broken-hearted porn…
pornography is not made up of old white men…nobody comes on them…
funny elbow porn/power walking porn/goiter porn/golfer porn/
restraining order porn/hearing aid porn/big house porn/
pimple blip porn/triple dip porn/blue chip porn/pink slip porn/
pornographic magic acts…*constitutionally protecting porn*
as if it were free speech means that there is a new way
in which we are legally chattel…porn born of Lesley Gore/
porn born of boredom/free range porn/Lorna Doone porn/
pornography bloopers/state trooper porn/handy fanny pack porn/
it's-hard-to-speak-freely-with-a-cock-in-my-mouth porn/
stackable porn/knickknack porn/flag and banner porn

CANNA

"The Barbie," a vaginal rejuvenation surgery,
promises to make the recipient smooth as plastic,
enticing as a waxed porn star
who, most probably a Deer Woman,

promises her viewers won't know she's faking it.
A Deer Woman's vulva has the daintiest lips,
naturally. Or via operation. Dear women,
are you Mares, Sheep, or Elephants?

Buffalo Women have the biggest, most luscious lips
like Georgia O'Keeffe's "Red Canna."
Mare Women, Sheep Women and Elephants
are better represented in her Series 1—Nos. 1-3.

Georgia O'Keeffe's "Red Canna"
suggests the rumbles of an earthquake orgasm
most evident in her Jack-in-the-Pulpits—Nos. 3-5.
Experienced by Raven Women and Crows,

slow-building earthquake orgasms
shake the whole body, wobble the bed.
Experienced by Fox Women and Wolves,
greased lightning orgasms come quickly then roll

to shake the whole body, wobble the bed.
Antelope Women and Cats have even reported
nipplegasms that come sporadically then roll
down their stomachs and legs.

All women have reported
they need their labia to feel pleasure spread
down their stomach and legs, but surgeons say
Shamed women will go under the knife.

Women need their labia to feel pleasure
but can also be humiliated, one body part at a time.
If you shame them, women will go under the knife.
First breast implants, now facelifts for the vulva.

Woman can be humiliated, one body part at a time—
porn went from big screen, to VCR, to computer.
First breast implants, now facelifts for the vulva
and waxing so viewers can see everything up close.

When porn went from big screen to computer
naked women shrank and so did their body parts.
Then came wax so viewers could see up close
what is naturally covered with hair.

Naked women shrink and so do their body parts
through dieting, treadmills, and lipo.
What is naturally covered with hair?
A woman's head, armpits, and legs.

Through dieting, treadmills, and lipo,
she might forget who she actually is.
A woman's head, armpits, legs,
and mons pubis become an emotional jungle.

She might forget who she actually is—
convinced her body needs to be tamed,
her mons pubis a jungle. Surgery
leaves her nipples and clitoris numb.

But accepting her body as wild
makes a woman feel enticing as a pulsar,
her nipples and clitoris become
celestial, exploding stars. Nothing like a doll's.

THE TENANTS OF FEMINISM

When the interviewer mishears "tenets"
I know my gals are not in a villa,
never mind the United States Senate.

My heroines crowd in drab tenements,
their image scaring even Attila
the Hun. The interviewer hears "tenants"—

bad asses, public housing. Bob Bennett
wakes sweaty from a nightmare, Guerilla
Girls rushing the United States Senate;

Gloria Steinem, bell hooks, and Joan Jett
stuffing manifestos in manila
mailers. The interviewer hears "tenants,"

sees kitchens where women cook venomous
dishes. His lady smells of vanilla,
minding their house, not the U.S. Senate.

My principles are not set in cement,
nor are they adrift on a flotilla.
I call upon all feminist "tenants"—
Steer your U-Hauls to the U.S. Senate.

READING

Sometimes I read pages of books without retaining anything.
I am thinking about my own drama and caesura
until I come across a word like "creosote," which seems familiar
but I have to look up. When I go to the dictionary, I realize
I am wondering who will bury me and where,
going over the time I was almost hit by a car on A1A.
It was dark, and he'd left me in the parking garage
saying, "I'll go ahead and get us a table." He meant
inside of Le Tub where there was always a long wait.
I stood in front of the Master Meter with my fistful of coins.
"OK," I said. What if that had been the end, that flattened smack, of me?
He would have looked up from the menu to the sirens—
their wail and red pulsing light—and it might have taken him
a moment to realize I was the one on the ground.
The thing about reading is that your mind might wander
to imagine the author sitting long enough
and silent enough to recall such a moment, so intimate
she never even mentioned it to her date.
The driver who almost hit me had forgotten
to turn on his headlights. And what about the intimacy
of writing itself? Each finger pad on a key, or the pen's whisper
into paper. What makes us do it, relive instead of live, go back
and forward in time? It's like dancing
to empty chairs in an empty room of a closed bar,
your shimmery ghost there long after you've left.
Only a few people will come to the dive
where you once danced, or turn to the page
where you left some marks, look at the words you wrote.

Fewer still will read them. Then a mixture
of vanity and humility if a stranger understands.
Or looks up a word she'd forgotten she knew.

MAYBE YOUR EAST VILLAGE WAS BETTER THAN MINE: A BRAIDED POEM

You had *Hair* on Broadway with naked actors
while we had the tame movie version
with Beverly D'Angelo and Treat Williams,

but you can never take the original *Evita* from us,
with Mandy Patinkin and Patti LuPone,
the former who now plays Saul on *Homeland*,

the latter who appears in the third season of *Girls*
as a fake spokesperson for an osteoporosis drug.
You are a baby boomer with a pension plan

and tricked out Winnebago. We are Gen X
filled with anxiety about the dying seas,
even though there's a five year span (1961-1966)

that's up for grabs. Those like myself, born in 1961,
can claim to be the youngest of boomers which is why
the "we" sometimes includes you and other times

not. We had Claire Danes as Angela in *My So-Called Life*,
but Gen Y has Claire Danes as Carrie Mathison
and Temple Grandin. *Homeland* and *Girls*

are for their generation, though we watch too.
Hulu pop-ups mock our age—Latisse to treat
"inadequate eyelash" growth, Swiffer WetJet,

and Astroglide. Gen Y-ers, also known as
the Millennials, have a film version in which Madonna
plays Evita and Antonio Banderas, Ché.

By the time *Rent* came along, I was too adult
to get it, even though I was still living
in Alphabet City just like the characters. I thought

the boring white guy narrator was exploiting
his colorful neighbors, but hadn't I done
the same thing? My early odes were to Felix,

the homeless man to whom I brought leftovers, writing
myself as a secular Mother Teresa. We were jealous,
we'll admit, when fellow Nuyorican poet Reg E. Gaines

received a Tony nomination for *Bring in 'da Noise,*
Bring in 'da Funk, but the play was so great
we saw it twice. We had *Hairspray* with Divine

and Rikki Lake, but they have *Hairspray* with John Travolta
and Nikki Blonsky. You had Baltimore riots
and they have Baltimore riots. We all have police brutality

and real war. We had Vietnam and they have
Iraq and Afghanistan, for which women can enlist.
Your brothers had shellshock, ours flashbacks, and now they

have PTSD. We had Elton John's "Philadelphia Freedom,"
but they have Elton John's *Lion King*.
We had Cyndi Lauper's "She Bop,"

but they have Cyndi Lauper's "True Colors"
in a Kodak commercial and later *Kinky Boots*.
Cyndi Lauper danced the streets of the Lower East Side

to make her "Girls Just Want to Have Fun" video
two summers before I moved there when Madonna
was buying yogurt at the same bodega where I

would later buy mine. We had poverty and they have poverty
with the spinoff T-shirt *Girls Just Want to Have Funds*.
By the time *Glee* and *Smash* came along

we were ready to join AARP. You had Quaaludes
and LSD. We had coke and crack addicts on the stoop.
You had political protests and we had crime waves—

one friend stabbed and another shot. They
have Ritalin, Oxy, and Xanax. You had rent control
and we had slum lords. They stay home

or sometimes move to Williamsburg or Red Hook.
You had girdles and long line bras. We had anorexia
and bulimia. They have plastic surgery and Spanx.

We had *The Brady Bunch* and they did too
because of Nickelodeon and *The Brady Bunch Movie.*
You had the Beatles and we did too because of Dick Clark

and oldies radio. They even have the Beatles
through "Revolution" in the Nike commercial.
We had The Jackson Five's "ABC" and Michael Jackson's

"Thriller." They have Michael Jackson's
child abuse allegations, his death by propofol,
and hologram. We had Pippi Longstocking

selling us self-reliance and they have Wendy
selling them burgers. You had braids, we had
French braids, and they have hair extensions.

All your Annies were white and so were ours.
Same with our Cinderellas—but they have Brandy
and Quvenzhané Wallis. All our movie couples

were pretty much the same color except in *To Sir with Love*
but we never got to see Lulu's crush bloom—not because of race,
but because of the student/teacher line which couldn't

be crossed. The night before I taught my first composition class
I was so nervous I got drunk at Area, a club you said
was better in your day before AIDS and skyrocketing

real estate. I danced with my friends then kissed a stranger.
The next morning he sat in the first row leering.
He stood near me in the elevator and told me

I smelled good until I started taking the five flights
of stairs. After a few weeks he dropped out—
maybe as a courtesy, maybe he was bad

at taking tests. Looking back at my rosters at Baruch,
I taught four people named Jennifer Lopez.
J Lo would have been there in those years,

but I don't remember anyone who seemed like her,
though does any celebrity truly seem
like their famous image in real life?

J Lo is only eight years younger than I am,
but now my students can be thirty years younger
or more. We both had moist thatches of hair, but they have

vajayjays and wax. Five years before *The Vagina
Monologues,* I let an editor change the title of my second
book to *The Woman with Two Vaginas*, the name

of one of the poems. He thought readers would think it
hilarious, but soon I was in a mess, promptly banned
and censored. My father had a nightmare I was shamed

on *The Phil Donahue Show* and relatives were calling him
asking where he and my mother had gone wrong.
We had Phil Donahue and they have Oprah.

You had feminism and we had feminism,
but we can't say our feminism was better than theirs,
can we? When we were in college, there wasn't even a term

for sexual harassment. So there was nothing to do
about the lit professors, their pregnant wives at home,
who tried to kiss us in their offices. Or the bosses

who squeezed our knees in break rooms
wanting to know why we didn't smile more.
Your harassment was worse than our harassment,

I'll admit, and it was even worse for our mothers
and grandmothers born in the Silent Generation
and the G. I. Generation and the generations before that.

All of us project ourselves onto the perils of Generation Z
and the end of the alphabet, just like all of us
can imagine the witch who came before, stripped

of her clothes—her head, legs, and pubis shaved
as the patriarchy believed a woman braided a man's fate
in her hair. She met her inquisitor walking backwards

so she couldn't give him the evil eye. Maybe your
East Village was indeed better than mine,
the avant-garde gasping its last breath

when Kmart came to Astor Place.
Her village had survived the Black Plague.
Hard to believe just three hundred years ago,

her children watched her burn at the stake.
I wish I could have seen *Hair* on Broadway,
those twenty seconds when actors stood naked

behind a scrim, chanting "beads, flowers, freedom,
and happiness." I've always wanted
to step back, but just a little bit, in time.

FOR WICKEDARY MARY

MARY DALY

(OCTOBER 16, 1928–JANUARY 3, 2010)

SAFETY PANTOUM

after Eve Ensler

The ones who save us are the ones killing us.
Religion, corporations, the military, and cops
all promise a better future, free from evil.
The mammogram machine radiates

religion, corporations, the military, and cops,
our breasts on cold metal plates.
The mammogram machine radiates.
But don't worry, you're safe, says the technician.

Our breasts on cold metal plates,
we say we've read that exposure causes cancer.
Don't worry, you're safe, says the technician.
The benefits far outweigh the risks.

We ask, *But doesn't exposure cause cancer?*
In 1775, chimneysweeps got scrotal cancer.
The risks far outweighed the benefits
for those boys diagnosed with cancer.

In 1775, chimneysweeps got scrotal cancer
from soot. Other carcinogens now
for those diagnosed with cancer—
tobacco, asbestos, tanning beds.

We've gone from soot to other carcinogens—
Dow chemicals, gasoline, the coloring agent in Coke,
tobacco, asbestos, tanning beds,
Monsanto's Roundup weed-killer.

Dow chemicals, gasoline, Coke's caffeine,
hormone replacement therapy, BPA water bottles,
and Monsanto's Roundup weed-killer
all make life easier. Giving up to

hormone replacement therapy and BPA water bottles
may rid you of hot flashes and night sweats,
make life easier. Giving in to
authority means you can always blame

your hot flashes and night sweats
on the military industrial complex. Religious
authority means you can always blame
God, yourself, or a nebulous enemy made up by

the military industrial complex. Religions
all promise a better future, free from evil,
God, yourself, or a nebulous made-up enemy.
The ones who save us are the ones killing us.

OUR LADY OF THE MILK

after Catherine Opie's "Self Portrait/Nursing"

what is a mother if not animal, suckling
her son, blue veins/vines
curling from her nipple/rose

blue tattoo wound (as in coiled)/
wound (as in bruise)
around her forearm

blue veins at baby's temple, mother
his first mystic meal, ancient
expression, expressing milk

mother, fading pervert—
she can't be both acceptable and not—
and her divine unmarked baby

litter, liter, tits and titter
what will we tell our sons
about Iraq and Syria

Seriously   what did
Mary, Our Lady
of the Milk, tell Jesus

about bonding and bondage,
latching on, latch key kids,
weaning, a trickling stream

Zeus placed baby Hercules
on Hera's breasts
as she slept   when she woke,

startled, she tossed the infant
from her chest, which squirted
the Milky Way

what is a mother if not human, marked
by freckles and tan lines,
cheeks flushed,

plush breasts,
her ambition, her past,
and chapped hands

in the Roman Empire
a mother dripped milk
onto her fingernail

the drop was supposed to
stay intact   not too thick
not too thin

Goldilocks, golden boy,
mother's calm face
belies her ache

the frozen peas
she'll put on her breasts
to numb the throbbing

mother, fading pervert—
yes, she can be both acceptable and not—
domestication, domestic bliss

Betty Friedan noted
post World War II women
romanticized domesticity

before that, Darwin noted the ears
of domesticated animals
relaxed and drooped

look at baby's perfect ear,
mother's perfect ear,
two bass clefs

the opera of humanity
between them
no housewife   no wolf

half of American women surveyed
think breastfeeding in public
is gross

but all endorse
our gross
domestic product

the son rests
his toes in the crook
of mother's elbow

she won't tell him yet
how he really got here
the blood and the shit

her wailing that day
of his birth
and how pain waned

like the cuttings,
the trimming of the grass/
the blades on her skin

the need to push
forward—conform and not—
history, her story,

libretto and folk song,
the music of the spheres/
the music of queers

what is a mother if not goddess,
her body round as the moon,
a berry, the equator, a compass

the mother wore him
like a backpack
but in the front

until her spine ached
until her feet started to swell
and there he was

the top of his head,
her crowning   he wore
his mother like a crown

DISTINGUISHED

There are poems and there are Poems,
Catholic people and catholic people,
chewing ice and really chewing ice to the irritation
of those nearest you. They say chewing ice is a sign
of sexual frustration, but who hasn't
chewed ice during deeply satisfying sex?
There is sex and there is Sex.
There are gums and there are gumballs.
There are professors and there are Distinguished Professors.
When they grade comp papers these days,
they distinguish a student's errors from her mistakes.
There are mistakes and there are big mistakes,
like marrying the wrong person or starting a war
in the wrong country. There are errors
and there are eras—Big Band, Vietnam, and Disco,
all of which are suitable subjects
for a poem and perhaps even a Poem.
There are subjects and there are objects,
and you know which one you are.

SNAKE PANTOUM

Once the snake was like the moon.
When a reptile shed its skin it seemed reborn,
becoming a symbol of eternal life.
The cobra was an early hieroglyph for "goddess".

When a reptile shed its skin it seemed reborn.
If there were no snakes, eels and dragons
stood in for the cobra, an early hieroglyph for "goddess."
One Cobra Goddess was a Lady of Spells.

If there were no snakes, eels, or dragons,
people imagined a feathered serpent.
One Cobra Goddess, the Lady of Spells,
may have used actual snakes for divination.

Wherever people imagined a feathered serpent,
they could also see the Ouroboros, tail in mouth,
using it as a sign of immortality, for divination.
Snakes coming out of nostrils meant clairvoyance

also seen in the Ouroboros, tail in mouth.
Medusa's snake-hair meant rebirth, menstruation
while snakes coming out of nostrils meant clairvoyance.
Goddess Una created the world with a rainbow snake.

Medusa's snake-hair meant rebirth, menstruation.
Elsewhere the first earth mother had a snake in her belly.
Goddess Una created the world with a rainbow snake,
the male sexual energy that lived inside her.

Elsewhere the first mother had a snake in her belly,
or she was a snake with a human head, female
and male sexual energy that lived in her,
as she created the first humans on Earth.

Before she was turned into a Gorgon—female
and vain and dangerous—she was purposeful
as she created the first humans on Earth.
A cobra looped around Isis's crown.

So when did the snake become dangerous, purposeful
in corrupting Eve in the Garden of Eden?
When did the cobra looped around Isis's crown
become a demon, a slithering Satan?

Corruption began with Eve in the Garden of Eden,
where a women's knowledge was equated with evil,
where a goddess became a demon, and Satan,
a foe so powerful, snakes have been maligned ever since.

When a women's knowledge is equated with evil,
there's nowhere to go but guilt,
a foe so powerful, women have been maligned ever since—
snake charmers, dragon ladies, old birds.

When there's nowhere to go but guilt,
women become eternally maligned—
snake charmers, dragon ladies, old birds.
Once the snake was like the moon.

SCALDING CAULDRON

Calling all Cosmic, Counterclock-Wise, Crackpot Crones who denounce docility, doublethink, and the domains of dummies. Our dragon eyes open, we exalt emotion, elixirs, and all elemental spirits. Our Foremothers forecasted the forests would be finished off, that feeble fembots would fall for fabricated fables. And here we are—at the future.

From the fortress of our fury, we begin this gyromancy (a practice in which a poet/witch seeks divination from a walk around the alphabet, taking note of the letters upon which she stumbles). Calling all Goddesses and Goofballs, Glamorous Grammarians, Giggling Gaggles of Geniuses, Gorgons and Gossips, Gyno-centric Gals, Heathens, Harpies, and Hags to come along and make this hexing hike. In this Intercourse of Individual Incarnations, may we intervene and influence junkies (ourselves?) addicted to joyless joists and other junk. On this journey, may we kick-start Kinship, put the kibosh on lecherous leeches and their laws, embrace the labyrinth of our lunacy, smash our mirrors.

May we maze our way through amazement, moon-wise, naming and renaming what has been misnamed. Calling all Nags and Nag-gnostics, Nag-noteworthy Nixes, and Nymphs. Calling all Outsiders, Ogres, those who check "Other," those from Otherworldly places, those Overlooked, and Old Maid Outercourse Pilgrims. Together we will chant, *Piss off—passive voice*. (A woman was not raped. Someone raped a woman.)

Calling all Pagans, Pixies, Prideful Prudes, Philosophers, Queens, and Quacks to rage and reverse, writing our Recourse to remember and reinvent our very syntax/sin-tax. Let's speckle the cracks with our sparkling cackles. Let's scold and scald. Let's *be* Skalds—poets who write of heroic deeds. Calling all Sisters, Sinners, Spinsters, Shrewd Shrews, Seers and Self-Realized Sirens. Calling all Soothsayers and Sinister Sprites, Shape-shifters and Separatists who cast spells.

Take a trek through this untidy alphabet. There will be toads and tidal time, the third ear and third eye. Traverse through unconventionality, where virtue and vice collide. Virgins and Vixens may experience vertigo, new to such wanderlust/wonderlust in this Wickedary. XX for kisses, XX for dead cartoon eyes. How we yearn at this zero hour.

(Where did you trip? Where did you fall? Please plan your augury accordingly.)

Our scalding cauldron is an abecedarian aquarium, boundless bubbles be-musing and be-monstering. We needn't stay one course: Recourse/Shulie Firestone; Intercourse/Andrea Dworkin; or Outercourse/Mary Daly, of course.

THE END IS COMING

Donna says she won't evacuate. Instead
she'll sit in her backyard, under the mango tree
with a cup of tea and think about nothing
but drinking that tea, becoming one with the tea,
until she is underwater or a chunk of debris
plops on her head and knocks her out.
I believe I will need some kind of help,
but I live alone and probably will be alone
when it happens. If I still have any battery,
I will listen to a "Feel Better Fast" podcast
on iTunes. It's better to visualize
while lying down, so I'll be on my couch
or on a cot in a shelter or maybe holding on tight
in a whirling hammock. A voice in my ear buds
will instruct me how to breathe and I will try
not to think of all the people in Bangladesh
sinking to their deaths or the farmers
killing themselves or the climate-change scientists,
their cold comfort of *I told you so.* I will try
not to think of the billionaire Koch brothers
in some bunker—I will try not to rage
as palms uproot and the wind blows me into something
sharp and concrete. I will finally give up
and *let those thoughts run in and out,*
send white light to my family members,
especially the littlest ones. I'll send white light
to those big dumb manatees who circled
the nuclear reactor because it made the water
so warm then realize I am a big dumb manatee
myself, drawn to Floridian weather

despite the costs. Then when the voice says,
What will this matter in a year from now,
a week from now? Will it really even matter
tomorrow? I will laugh my last breath
though it's no laughing matter.
It's just the way some of us cope.

HUMANITY 101

I was on my way to becoming a philanthropist,
or the president, or at least someone who gave a shit,
but I was a nontraditional student
with a lot of catching up to do. I enrolled in Humanity 101
(not to be confused with the Humanities,
a whole separate department). When I flunked
the final exam, my professor suggested
I take Remedial Humanity where I'd learn the basics
that I'd missed so far. I may have been a nontraditional student
but I was a traditional person, she said.

So I took Remedial Humanity, which sounds like an easy A,
but believe me, it was actually quite challenging.
There were analogy questions such as
Paris Hilton is to a rich U.S. suburban kid
as a U.S middle-class kid is to
1. a U.S poverty-stricken kid
2. a U.S. kid with nothing in the fridge
or
3. a Third World kid with no fridge at all.

We were required to write essays about the cause of war—
was it a phenomenon? Was it our lower animal selves?
Was it economics? Was it psychological/sexual/religious?
We had to bend down to talk to a homeless person
slouched against a building. We didn't necessarily have to
give them money or food, but we had to say something like
How are you? or *What is your favorite song?*

We took field trips to nursing homes, prisons,
daycare centers. We stood near bedsides
or sat on the floor to color. I almost dropped out.
I wanted to change my major. The professor
thought I should stick it out, that I could make it,
if I just escaped for an hour a day blasting music
from my ear buds or slumping in front of the TV.
I said, *But that's just it. Now I see humanity everywhere,*
even on sitcoms, even in pop songs,
even in beer commercials. He closed his door
and showed me the scars under his shirt
where he had been stabbed. He said I had to assume
everyone had such a wound, whether I could see it or not.

He said I had to write a treatise on detachment.

CASTRATI OF THE EIGHTEENTH CENTURY

Their voices—part lark, part angel, part ghost—
haunted the Sistine Chapel Choir
where parishioners became engrossed,

ecstatic as they swallowed the host.
Castrated men best mimicked desire,
their voices—part lark, part angel, part ghost.

Their scrotums smashed or snipped as children, most
boys bled to death, never to acquire
grueling voice lessons or become engrossed

in church politics or opera. Toasts
of the town, "lucky" castrati inspired
androgyny—part lark, part angel, part ghost.

Long live the little knife! Women would boast
of trysts with men who wore women's attire.
Titillated opera buffs were engrossed.

The church killed one hundred thousand poster
boys for pain. Those who lived couldn't sire
children, part lark, part angel, part ghost.
And centuries later we're still engrossed.

WHAT CHILD IS THIS?

In 1871, it was common to parody evolution.
Women plainly had beards and big whiskers at first
was sung to the tune of "Greensleeves,"
a song I knew growing up as "What Child is This?"

Women plainly had beards and big whiskers at first
while the man supplied milk when the baby was nursed.
Growing up I knew the song as "What Child is This?"
I played it on the accordion at Christmas.

Now a man *can* supply milk when the baby is nursed,
if you see gender and parenthood as social constructs.
I played the accordion at Christmas
before I grew breasts or knew who Darwin was.

If you see gender and parenthood as social constructs,
Jesus's wounds look like vulvas. For me, God was male
before I grew breasts or knew who Darwin was.
"What Child is This?" rang from secular ice cream trucks.

Jesus's wounds look like vulvas. For me, God was male
but kind of creepy since he could see my every move.
"Greensleeves" rang from secular ice cream trucks.
I wondered if God thought I was fat as I slurped a cone.

Santa was also creepy since he could see my every move
and it was a relief to find out he didn't exist so I could stop
wondering if God thought I was fat as I slurped a cone.
It was a relief to come from a single-celled organism,

a relief to find out God didn't exist so I could stop
going to church and sleep late on Sundays.
It was a relief to come from a single-celled organism,
to learn my periods weren't really a curse.

My parents still went to church, but I slept late on Sundays
then read Nancy Friday and Betty Friedan
and learned my period wasn't really a curse.
In India, menstruating girls were given money and feasts!

After I read Nancy Friday and Betty Friedan,
I couldn't see priests as anything but oppressive.
In India, menstruating girls were given money and feasts!
But here at mass, Father Billy said we were unclean.

I couldn't see priests as anything but oppressive.
I vowed when I had a boyfriend he'd earn his "red wings"
because here at mass, Father Billy said we were unclean.
Although I refused my confirmation,

I vowed when I had a boyfriend he'd earn his "red wings."
Hell's Angels went down on their menstruating girlfriends!
Although I refused to go to confession,
I confess I was still a little concerned with heaven and hell.

Hell's Angels went down on their menstruating girlfriends!
Maybe I'd meet one of those bikers someday
from a gang that conflated heaven and hell,
a guy so tough he was unafraid of a woman's blood.

But where could I meet one of those bikers now?
I wondered if there was a dirt bike aficionado in junior high,
a guy so tough he was unafraid of a woman's blood.
In truth, even I was a little afraid of my blood.

Instead I fell for the tender guy in junior high.
Trying to be edgy, I dressed as a pregnant nun for Halloween.
I never gave my guy a chance, afraid of my own blood.
I was still superstitious, afraid to be struck by lightning.

I dressed as a pregnant nun for Halloween
and Mrs. Dubois refused to give me a Hershey's.
I was afraid to be struck by lightning
as she quoted John 8:23, *The truth will set you free.*

When Mrs. Dubois refused to give me a Hershey's
I summoned Gloria Steinem—
The truth will set you free
but first it will piss you off.

Gloria Steinem said I wasn't going to hell.
I sang *I am woman, hear me roar...*
In truth, I was really pissed off
at the world, fueled by teenage hormones.

I sang *I am woman, hear me roar...*
then my uncle sang *I am sleeping, hear me snore.*
The world seemed fueled by teenage hormones
and I leapt into political debates with grownups.

My uncle sang *I am sleeping, hear me snore,*
ruining Helen Reddy's pop manifesto.
I leapt into political debates with grownups.
In 1975, no girl could afford to parody feminism.

PILGRIMS

In June 2012, Mecca had the hottest downpour
in earth's history—rain at 109 degrees. I had just finished
replacing my last old light bulb with the new expensive twisty kind
which I now learn contains mercury,
                              that beautiful dollop
that once rolled out from a broken thermometer when I was a child,
its elusive silver shimmer. I had a fever, now the planet has a fever.
I don't remember how
                    my mother disposed of the mercury,
but we are supposed to open the windows if we break
one of these new bulbs, wear gloves for the clean up.
The earth's fever will not break.
                              Feverish agribusiness—
no crop rotation, overgrazing. *It is difficult to get a man
to understand something, when his salary depends on
his not understanding it,* wrote Upton Sinclair.
                                        Everyone
at the dinner parties I go to agrees—we have to do something.
Sincerity. Irony. It doesn't really matter which. *Thieves
of pennies and dimes…put out of the way
                              by the swindlers
of millions.* Upton Sinclair, again. Pilgrims to the holy city
looked up, surprised by the warm drops, by a breeze coming in
from the Red Sea where ancient turtles slogged through crude.

AMERICAS

When the new board took over the condo, they fired the ground's crew and hired new workers through a company that cost less, that didn't give out any benefits. Joe, my favorite doorman, the one with Parkinson's, had to cash in his stash of gold coins to pay his rent. He had memorized my phone number since I was the tenant who received the most packages, mostly books. I wrote Joe a reference letter, and finally he was hired to patrol a park. It was hard for him to be on his feet, in the hot Florida sun, but still, he called to say he was grateful.

Until the new board, Enrique took care of the garbage and washed the hallway floors. Once I hired him afterhours to put in a new showerhead. He had his own yellow toolbox and wiped up his footprints with a bunch of paper towels as he backed out the door. *I'll get it. No worries,* I said. The shower had still been wet from earlier in the day. He bent at the waist. *No, no, lady, this is my job.* And then, with all the other workers, one day he was gone.

I saw him a year later at the university where I teach. *Are you taking classes?* I asked. *You know I was sacked, right?* Enrique said. I nodded, *I wrote a letter to the board, but it didn't do any good.* Enrique unzipped his backpack to show me a towel and a bar of green soap swaddled in Saran Wrap. *I'm here to take a shower.* He used the facilities in the gym since no one checked IDs. He was living in his car and slept behind Wal-Mart with a bunch of other homeless people. I asked for his number, not knowing what I would say if I called. He still had his phone but no service. I gave him a twenty, which was all I had on me. We both stood there, in our own Americas. He walked away first.

I saw Joe once again in the Publix parking lot—a triangle of white sunblock on his nose, sweat stains under the armpits of what was his new khaki uniform. He asked about my friends who'd visited me at the condo—he even remembered their names. He asked about my neighbor who had since moved. We talked about all the foreclosures, the latest hurricanes, cuts in the parks department, which meant Joe now was mostly walking on sweltering cement. I came home to take a shower where Enrique, fully clothed, once stood, his silver wrench on the bathroom counter, open like a mouth.

FILLING STATION, 2012

after Elizabeth Bishop (Great Village, Nova Scotia)

Oh, but it is shiny!
—this little filling station
taking Visa, selling Mountain Dew,
the last station for 62.8 kilometers.
There's even a red-handled squeegee
for your windshield!

No one works outside,
except for the blue self-serve tanks.
A customer pops
her gas cap, swipes a debit card,
drags the hose, and tilts the obscene nozzle
into her car's hole. (The place
is not a family station anymore.)

The workers inside wear blue fleece
jackets, the ESSO-SO-SO-SO cans
replaced by Red Bull, Doritos,
H2Go!, and Gourmet Ice Slushies,
orange and purple, churning in their machines.
A sign says *Try our coffee combos!*
The Lotto is 7 million this week.

There is color everywhere—
behind the counter, a display
of Cherry Boxes, toys and fireworks
for "instant" parties. A spinning rack of pinkish
Mother's Day cards. No comic books, but Superhitz
DVDs for rent—*Hangover Part II,*
Soul Surfer, X-Men, and *Avatar.*

Why the *Dawn of the Dead* movie poster
with zombies in shadow
against the setting pumpkin sun?
(The tagline—When there's no more room
in hell, the dead will walk the earth.)

Somebody signed the contract.
Somebody drills into the ground
under the sea. Somebody
writes a press release
and makes sure each gas station
is bright and clean with an attached
automated car wash to blast away our sins.
Somebody fools us all.

RECYCLING

after Gwendolyn Brooks (from "garbageman: the man with the orderly mind")

We, who know it is
probably too late, do it anyway. Our light
bulbs (compact fluorescent) look enough
like pigs' tails to remind us (if
we'd forgotten) of our piggy-ness. Our hands
sort the glass from plastic, cardboard in
plastic (more plastic!) bins. Clumsy
is our language. "Green" is also the frenzy
of money, our false flimsy
innocence, and our camouflage, whimsically
patterned, calling us to enlist.

THE THINGS THAT NEVER CAN COME BACK

As Dickinson writes *Childhood—some forms of Hope—the Dead.*
So religion, science, and comic books
do their best to close the loop, to see the seasons
as proof of something circular, that spring will follow

whatever obstacles religion, science, and comic books
find in their path. We tell ourselves fairy tales
as proof of something, that spring will follow—
a poisoned comb and coffin can't stop Snow White

from returning. We tell ourselves tales
of immortality. The cross didn't stop Jesus.
A poisoned comb and coffin didn't stop Snow White.
Walt Disney was actually cremated, despite rumors

of immortality. The cross didn't stop Jesus,
according to some. According to the Cryonics Institute,
Walt Disney was cremated, despite rumors
that he was frozen. But almost 300 others,

according to their families and the Cryonics Institute,
have undergone cryopreservation, their brains
resting, "dead" and frozen. These 300 others
believe that one day resuscitation will be possible.

Having undergone accidental cryopreservation,
dead Captain America returned from the Arctic years later
and readers believed his resuscitation possible.
Alaskan wood frogs, Eastern box turtles,

and Captain America came alive after cold winters.
Florida iguanas freeze at just 40 degrees, and, like
Alaskan wood frogs and Eastern box turtles,
they come back to life when it warms up.

Florida iguanas freeze at just 40 degrees, and, like
children falling out of bed, they fall out of trees,
startled, coming back to life when it warms up.
Benjamin Franklin wanted to come back to life—

like a child waking in bed, like a new tree leaf—
to see what his country would be like 100 years later.
Benjamin Franklin wanted to come back to life
though he thought men wicked, even with religion.

He worried what his country would be in 1890—
all wars, follies. He thought it better to cast dice than fight.
He wrote *If Men are so wicked as we now see them with Religion
what would they be if without it?*

All wars *are* follies. It is better to cast dice than fight—
but what about religious wars, the promise of glory?
What would soldiers be without it?
The dead are replaced with medals, headstones, parades

of an almost religious nature, the promise of glory.
Hope is a slogan, one we'll not soon fall for again.
The dead are replaced with medals, headstones,
and we look for our childhoods on eBay and YouTube.

Hope is a slogan, one we'll not soon fall for again.
The Millennium Seed Bank gathers up what is not yet extinct
as we look for our childhoods on eBay and YouTube.
Gone forever is the Golden Toad, Javan Tiger, Pyrenean Ibex.

The Millennium Seed Bank gathers up what is not yet extinct,
though we've already lost over 400 kinds of lettuce,
the Golden Toad and Javan Tiger. A Pyrenean Ibex
clone died from complications, despite "de-extinction" efforts.

Though we've already lost over 400 kinds of lettuce,
the Judean date palm came back after 2000 years.
Clones die from complications, despite "de-extinction" efforts,
but moss piglets seem to survive no matter what.

When the Judean date palm came back after 2000 years,
we wondered if death was just an ambulance to the future.
Moss piglets will survive no matter what—
environmental toxins, drought, and radiation.

What if death is an ambulance to the future?
We do our best to see the seasons, but the future may be
environmental toxins, drought, and radiation.
Some forms hold onto childhood, hold onto hope.

ACKNOWLEDGMENTS

Grateful acknowledgment is made to the editors and staff members of the magazines, chapbook, and anthologies in which poems from *Scald* first appeared:

American Poetry Review: "How Deep It Goes" (published with the title "Nature") and "Porn Poem (with Andrea Dworkin)"; *Boston Poetry:* "Memoir"; *Cog:* "Amazon" and "Extreme Villanelle"; *BuzzFeed:* "Rated R"; *Columbia Poetry Review:* "People-ing"; *The Common:* "Reader/Writer"; *Cossack Review:* "Reproduction Pantoum"; *Court Green:* "On the Occasion of Typing My First Email on a Brand-New Phone" and "Sex Dream" (published with the title "Sex"); *Five Points:* "Dogs"; *Heart:* "Americas"; *Green Mountains Review:* "Safety Pantoum" and "Maybe Your East Village Was Better Than Mine: A Braided Poem"; *International Literary Quarterly:* "Helen Hamilton Gardener's Brain," "Pilgrims," "Filling Station, 2012," and "Recycling"; *The Literary Review:* "Fornicating"; *Lunch:* "Bikini Kill Villanelle"; *Ocean State Review:* "Canna" and "Castrati of the Eighteenth Century"; *New Ohio Review:* "The Tenants of Feminism"; *Pilgrimage:* "Scalding Cauldron"; *Pittsburgh Poetry Review:* "What Child Is This?" and "The End Is Coming" (published with the title "The End"); *Ploughshares:* "Reading"; *Poet Lore:* "Darwinian Pantoum"; *Southern Review:* "Snake Pantoum" and "Humanity 101"; *Unsplendid:* "The Things That Never Can Come Back"; *Upstreet:* "Distinguished"; *Valley Voices: New York School and Diaspora: A Special Issue:* "The Immortal Jellyfish"

"Our Lady of the Milk" appears in *Storylines,* a chapbook published by the Guggenheim Museum in 2015 and on the website http://exhibitions.guggenheim .org/storylines/catherine-opie

"Fornicating" is reprinted in *The Best American Poetry 2015* (edited by Lehman and Alexie), and "Humanity" is reprinted in *The Best American Poetry 2016* (edited by Lehman and Hirsch).

"Recycling" is reprinted in *The Golden Shovel Anthology* (edited by Kahn et al., University of Arkansas Press, 2017).

With many thanks to the Guggenheim Foundation, Florida International University, The Elizabeth Bishop House, Stephanie Strickland, Ted McMahon, Arielle Greenberg, Kim Edwards, Mark Savage, and especially Ed Ochester. "Darwinian Pantoum" and "Snake Pantoum" owe much to *The Great Cosmic Mother: Rediscovering the Religion of the Earth* by Monica Sjoo and Barbara Mor. "Helen Hamilton Gardener's Brain" owes much to *From Eve to Evolution: Darwin, Science, and Women's Rights in Gilded Age America* by Kimberly A. Hamlin.